**BASS
REVISED EDITION**

J327	Book	6.50
J328	Compact Disc	10.00
J329	Book & CD	16.50

Jump Right In
the instrumental series

Richard F. Grunow
*Professor of Music Education
Eastman School of Music
of the University of Rochester*

Edwin E. Gordon
*Research Professor
University of South Carolina*

Christopher D. Azzara
*Associate Professor of Music Education
Eastman School of Music
of the University of Rochester*

Michael E. Martin
*School District of Haverford Township
Havertown, Pennsylvania*

STUDENT BOOK ONE

AN INSTRUMENTAL METHOD DESIGNED FOR DEVELOPING AUDIATION SKILLS AND EXECUTIVE SKILLS

Instrument	Bk 1	CD 1	Bk1 & CD	Bk 2	CD 2	Bk2 & CD	Solo Bk 1	Solo Bk 2	Solo Bk 3
Violin	J318	J319	J320	J330		J332	J169	J163	J218
Viola	J321	J322	J323	J333	J331	J334	J170	J164	J219
Cello	J324	J325	J326	J335		J336	J171	J165	J220
Bass	J327	J328	J329	J337		J338	J172	J166	J221
Recorder	J231	J232	J233	J247	J245CD	J245	J94	J149	J217

Revised Teacher's Guide for Strings Books 1 and 2 .... J317
Revised Teacher's Guide for Band Books 1 and 2 .... J315
JRI for Winds and Percussion (specify instrument)
Revised Teacher's Guide for Recorder J235
Solo Book 1–Writing (all instruments) J167
Solo Book 2–Writing (all instruments) J168
Solo Book 3–Writing (all instruments) J203
Composition Book 1 (all instruments) J249
GIA Heavy Duty Sporano Recorder M447
Concert Selections for Wind and Percussion (specify instrument)
JRI Video for Teachers J98
Parent's Guide J177

RECORDED SOLOS WITH ACCOMPANIMENTS

Cassette Bk 1:	Cassette Bk 2:	Cassette Bk 3:
J99	J148	J200
CD Bk 1:	CD Bk 2:	CD Bk 3:
J99CD	J148CD	J200CD

LISTENING

Simple Gifts	*Don Gato*	*You Are My Sunshine*
Cassette:	Cassette:	Cassette:
J229CS	J201CS	J199CS
CD:	CD:	CD:
J229CD	J201CD	J199CD

**GIA Publications, Inc.
7404 S. Mason Ave., Chicago, IL 60638**

ASSIGNMENT SCHEDULE

The teacher will specify the student's assignments. The student will insert the date and check (✓) underneath the date to indicate specific assignments. The *Home-Study Compact Disc* Track # is the same as the Item Number.

READ THE FOLLOWING	Page No.
A NOTE TO PARENTS AND STUDENTS	ii
PRACTICE TIPS	4
USE OF THE *HOME-STUDY COMPACT DISC*	5
PLAYING IN TUNE WITH THE *HOME-STUDY COMPACT DISC*	5
PARTS OF THE INSTRUMENT AND BOW	6
DEVELOPING POSTURE AND INSTRUMENT POSITION	6
FORMING THE BOW HOLD	7
RIGHT HAND PIZZICATO	7
PERFORMING ON THE D STRING - NO FINGERS DOWN	7
LEFT HAND POSITION	7

LISTEN TO THE HOME-STUDY COMPACT DISC AND FOLLOW THE DIRECTIONS FOR

Item/Track No.		Unit
1	Singing "Major Duple" a-Melody b-Bass Line	1-A
2	Accompaniment for Singing "Major Duple"	
3	Connected Style of Articulation	
4	Separated Style of Articulation	
5	Singing "Hot Cross Buns" a-Melody b-Bass Line	1-B
6	Accompaniment for Singing "Hot Cross Buns"	
7	Connected and Separated Styles of Articulation on the D String	
8	Singing "Minor Duple" a-Melody b-Bass Line	2-A
9	Accompaniment for Singing "Minor Duple"	
10	Tonal Patterns - Major - Tonic and Dominant - Neutral Syllable	
11	Tonal Patterns - Major - Tonic and Dominant - Tonal Syllables	
12	Melodic Patterns on D-DO and SO	
13	Singing "Mary Had a Little Lamb" a-Melody b-Bass Line	2-B
14	Accompaniment for Singing "Mary Had a Little Lamb"	
15	Connected and Separated Styles of Articulation on RE	
16	Melodic Patterns on D-DO and RE	
17	Rhythm Patterns - Duple - Macro and Microbeats - Neutral Syllable	
18	Rhythm Patterns - Duple - Macro and Microbeats - Rhythm Syllables	
19	Singing "Major Triple" a-Melody b-Bass Line	3-A
20	Accompaniment for Singing "Major Triple"	
21	Tonal Patterns - Minor - Tonic and Dominant - Neutral Syllable	
22	Tonal Patterns - Minor - Tonic and Dominant - Tonal Syllables	
23	Connected and Separated Styles of Articulations on MI	
24	Melodic Patterns on MI and RE	
25	Melodic Patterns on D-DO, RE, and MI	
26	Performance of "Hot Cross Buns"	

Copyright © 2002 by GIA Publications, Inc. 7404 South Mason Avenue, Chicago, IL 60638
International copyright secured. All rights reserved. Printed in the United States of America

Item/Track No.		DATE	DATE	DATE	DATE	DATE	DATE	DATE	DATE	DATE	DATE	DATE	DATE	DATE	DATE
27 - "Hot Cross Buns" - Accompaniment Only															
28 - Singing "Twinkle, Twinkle, Little Star" a-Melody b-Bass Line	3-B														
29 - Accompaniment for Singing "Twinkle, Twinkle, Little Star"															
30 - Rhythm Patterns - Triple - Macro/microbeats - Neutral Syllable															
31 - Rhythm Patterns - Triple - Macro/microbeats - Rhythm Syllables															
32 - Melodic Patterns on SO and MI															
33 - Melodic Patterns on D-DO, RE, MI, and SO															
34 - Patterns from "Mary Had a Little Lamb"															
35 - Performance of "Mary Had a Little Lamb"															
36 - "Mary Had a Little Lamb" - Accompaniment Only															
37 - Singing "Minor Triple" a-Melody b-Bass Line	4-A														
38 - Accompaniment for Singing "Minor Triple"															
39 - Melodic Patterns on MI and FA															
40 - Melodic Patterns on D-DO and SO															
41 - Melodic Patterns on SO and LA															
42 - Melodic Patterns on D-DO, RE, MI, FA, SO, and LA															
43 - Performance of "Twinkle, Twinkle, Little Star"															
44 - "Twinkle, Twinkle, Little Star" - Accompaniment Only															
45 - Melodic Patterns on G-DO and TI															
46 - Singing "Pierrot" a-Melody b-Bass Line	4-B														
47 - Accompaniment for Singing "Pierrot"															
48 - Melodic Patterns on G-DO, TI, and RE															
49 - Melodic Patterns on G-DO, TI, RE, and MI															
50 - Patterns from "Major Duple" - Connected Style															
51 - Patterns from "Major Duple" - Separated Style															
52 - Performance of "Major Duple"															
53 - "Major Duple" - Accompaniment Only															
54 - Singing "Go Tell Aunt Rhody" a-Melody b-Bass Line	5-A														
55 - Accompaniment for Singing "Go Tell Aunt Rhody"															
56 - Patterns from "Major Triple" - Connected Style															
57 - Patterns from "Major Triple" - Separated Style															
58 - Performance of "Major Triple"															
59 - "Major Triple" - Accompaniment Only															
60 - Singing "Down By the Station" a-Melody b-Bass Line	5-B														
61 - Accompaniment for Singing "Down By the Station"															
62 - Rhythm Patterns - Duple - Divisions - Neutral Syllable															
63 - Rhythm Patterns - Duple - Divisions - Rhythm Syllables															
64 - Melodic Patterns on C-DO, RE, and MI															
65 - Performance of "Pierrot"															
66 - "Pierrot" - Accompaniment Only															
67 - Singing "Lightly Row" a-Melody b-Bass Line	6-A														
68 - Accompaniment for Singing "Lightly Row"															
69 - Tonal Patterns - Major - Tonic, Dominant, Subdominant - Neutral Syllable															

	DATE	DATE	DATE	DATE	DATE	DATE	DATE	DATE	DATE	DATE	DATE	DATE	DATE	DATE
70 - Tonal Patterns - Major - Tonic, Dominant, Subdominant - Tonal Syllables														
71 - Melodic Patterns on D-DO, RE, MI, FA, and SO														
72 - Performance of "Go Tell Aunt Rhody"														
73 - "Go Tell Aunt Rhody" - Accompaniment Only														
74 - Singing "Triple Twinkle" a-Melody b-Bass Line 6-B														
75 - Accompaniment for Singing "Triple Twinkle"														
76 - "Down by the Station" - Accompaniment Only														
77 - Rhythm Patterns - Triple - Divisions - Neutral Syllable														
78 - Rhythm Patterns - Triple - Divisions - Rhythm Syllables														
79 - Singing "Minor Aunt Rhody" a-Melody b-Bass Line 7-A														
80 - Accompaniment for Singing "Minor Aunt Rhody"														
81 - Tonal Patterns - Minor - Tonic, Dominant, Subdominant - Neutral Syllable														
82 - Tonal Patterns - Minor - Tonic, Dominant, Subdominant - Tonal Syllables														
83 - "Lightly Row" - Accompaniment Only														
84 - Singing "Triple Pierrot" a-Melody b-Bass Line 7-B														
85 - Accompaniment for Singing "Triple Pierrot"														
86 - Rhythm Patterns - Duple - Elongations - Neutral Syllable														
87 - Rhythm Patterns - Duple - Elongations - Rhythm Syllables														
88 - Singing "Little Tom Tinker" a-Melody b-Bass Line 8-A														
89 - Accompaniment for Singing "Little Tom Tinker"														
90 - Singing "Baa, Baa, Black Sheep" a-Melody b-Bass Line 8-B														
91 - Accompaniment for Singing "Baa, Baa, Black Sheep"														
92 - Rhythm Patterns - Triple - Elongations - Neutral Syllable														
93 - Rhythm Patterns - Triple - Elongations - Rhythm Syllables														
94-97 Musical Enrichment - See page 47.														
98 - Tuning Your Instrument														

PRACTICE TIPS

Under typical circumstances, you should practice every day. When first learning to play an instrument, however, it is most effective if you practice for shorter periods of time. Two sessions of 10 to 15 minutes each day are better than one longer session. Although you will be able to practice for longer periods of time after the first several lessons, it will still be most beneficial if you continue practicing for two shorter sessions, as opposed to one longer session.

How you practice is more important than the length of time you practice. To establish goals for each practice session you should refer to the *Assignment Schedule* on pages 2 - 4, along with the information and illustrations on pages 5 - 7. It is also important to read carefully the guidelines for developing executive skills, which include posture, instrument position, bow hold, and left hand position.

USE OF THE HOME-STUDY COMPACT DISC

The *Home-Study Compact Disc* (CD) is an important part of *Jump Right In: The Instrumental Series*. The CD should be played on good equipment. If you do not have a CD player, ask your teacher if you may use one to practice with during the school day, or if you may borrow a CD player from the school or a music store until you obtain your own.

You will use the CD when you practice at home. During your lessons at school, your teacher will explain how to practice at home with your CD. Every item on the CD will be used to help you learn a specific assignment in this book, as explained on the *Assignment Schedule* on pages 2 - 4. For example, after the first lesson you will be asked to listen to the CD and follow the directions for Items 1, 2, 3, and 4. Listen to and follow the directions as many times as you wish. You may replay items on the CD as many times as necessary. Ask your teacher for permission, however, before you listen to items that have not been assigned.

When using the CD, you will typically want to review previous assignments. Perhaps there will be times when you will wish to start with the assignment given in your last lesson. In that case, simply call up the number of that item on the CD player. If you have the "repeat" option on your CD player, you may use it to repeat the item as many times as you wish.

Ask your teacher for help if you are having a problem with following the directions for *Use of the Home-Study Compact Disc*. Protect your CD when you are not practicing by storing it in the plastic sleeve included in this book.

PLAYING IN TUNE WITH THE HOME-STUDY COMPACT DISC

Although the speed of compact disc players is generally consistent, you may find that it is necessary to tune your instrument daily. Your teacher will help you tune your instrument for the first few lessons. Listen to directions for "Tuning Your Instrument" (Track 98 on the *Home Study Compact Disc*). Tuning can be accomplished by turning the machine pegs. (See Figures 1 and 2.) Except when playing with the accompaniments that are provided on the CD, you should ALWAYS REPEAT on your instrument AFTER you hear the musical example on the CD. DO NOT PERFORM on your instrument WITH what you are hearing on the CD.

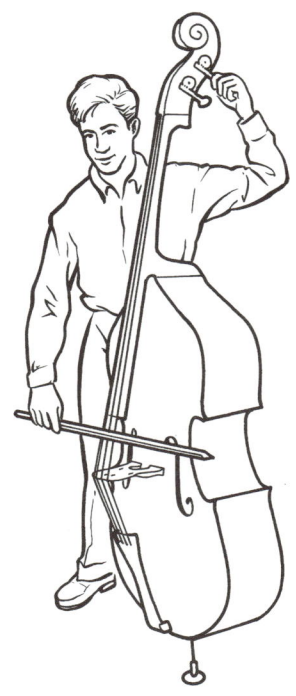

Figure 1.   **Figure 2.**

PARTS OF THE INSTRUMENT AND BOW

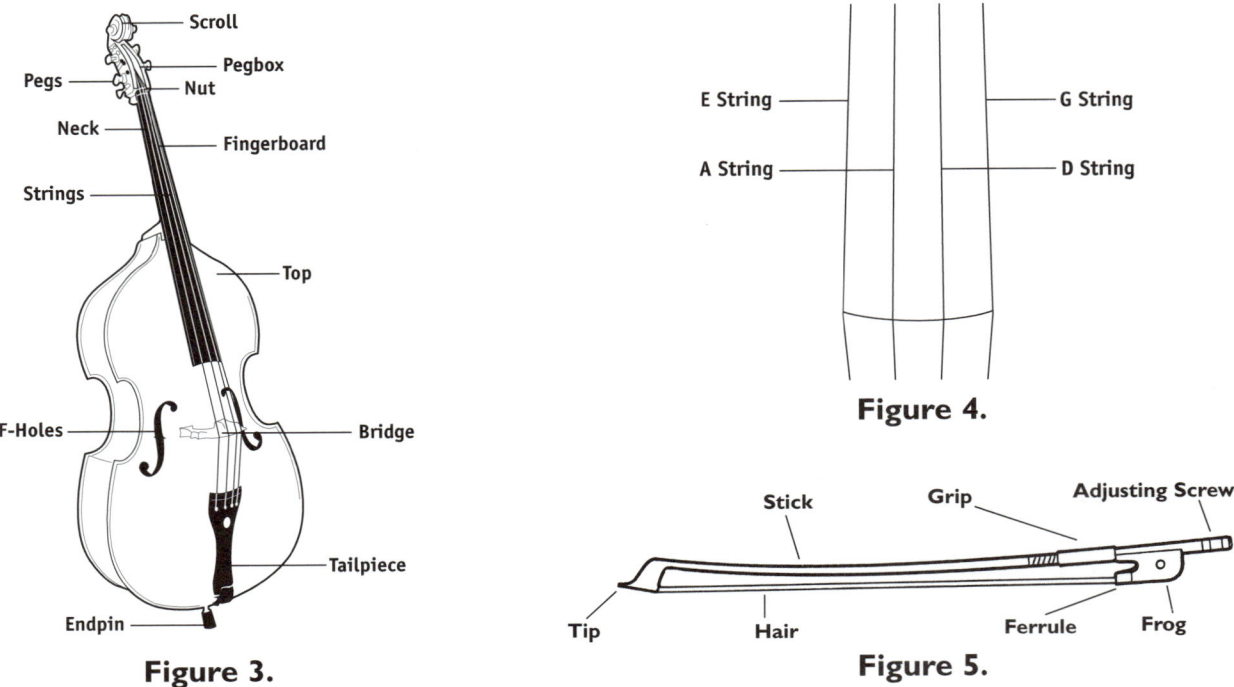

Figure 3.

Figure 4.

Figure 5.

DEVELOPING POSTURE AND INSTRUMENT POSITION

As a bassist, you may be practicing and performing in a standing position or while seated on a stool. Whether you are standing or seated, appropriate performance habits are dependent upon correct posture and instrument position. Your teacher will help you initially to adjust the endpin to the proper height.

Step 1 - Stand erect or sit erect on the front of the stool. Move your left foot slightly forward or elevate your left foot on a rung of the stool. Hold your bass at arm's length. See Figure 6.

Step 2 - Turn the bass slightly to the right and lean the bass back until it rests against the left side of your abdomen. See Figure 7.

Study Figures 8 and 9 for correct body posture and instrument position while sitting and standing.

Figure 6.

Figure 7.

Figure 8.

Figure 9.

FORMING THE BOW HOLD

FRENCH BOW

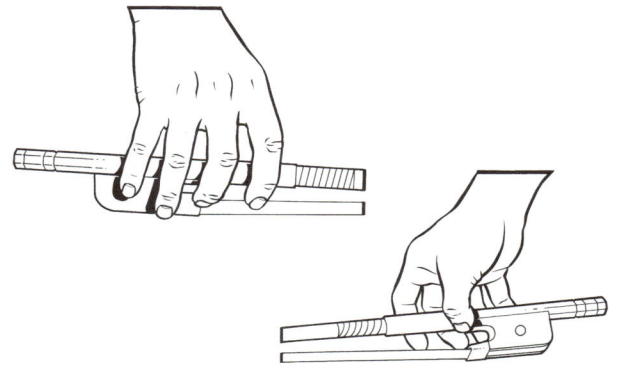

Figure 10.

GERMAN BOW

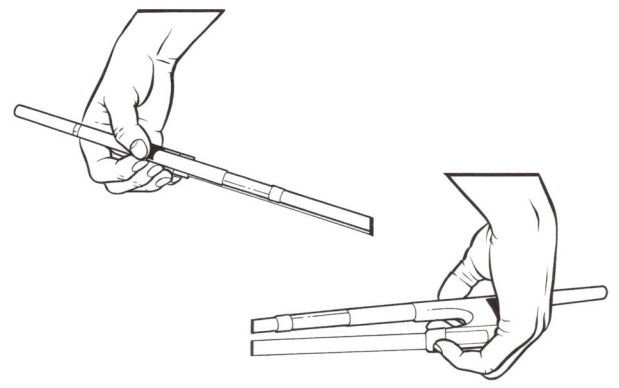

Figure 11.

RIGHT HAND PIZZICATO

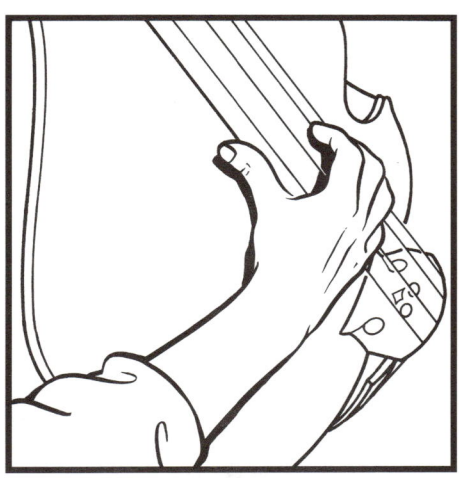

Figure 12.

PERFORMING ON THE D STRING - NO FINGERS DOWN

Figure 13.

LEFT HAND POSITION

Figure 14.

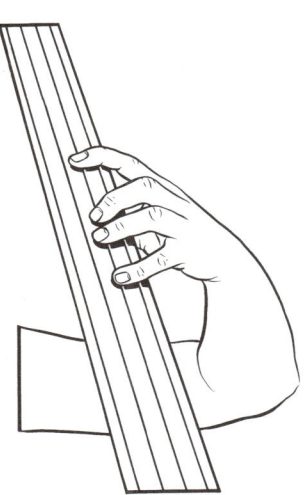

Figure 15.

BASS FINGERINGS

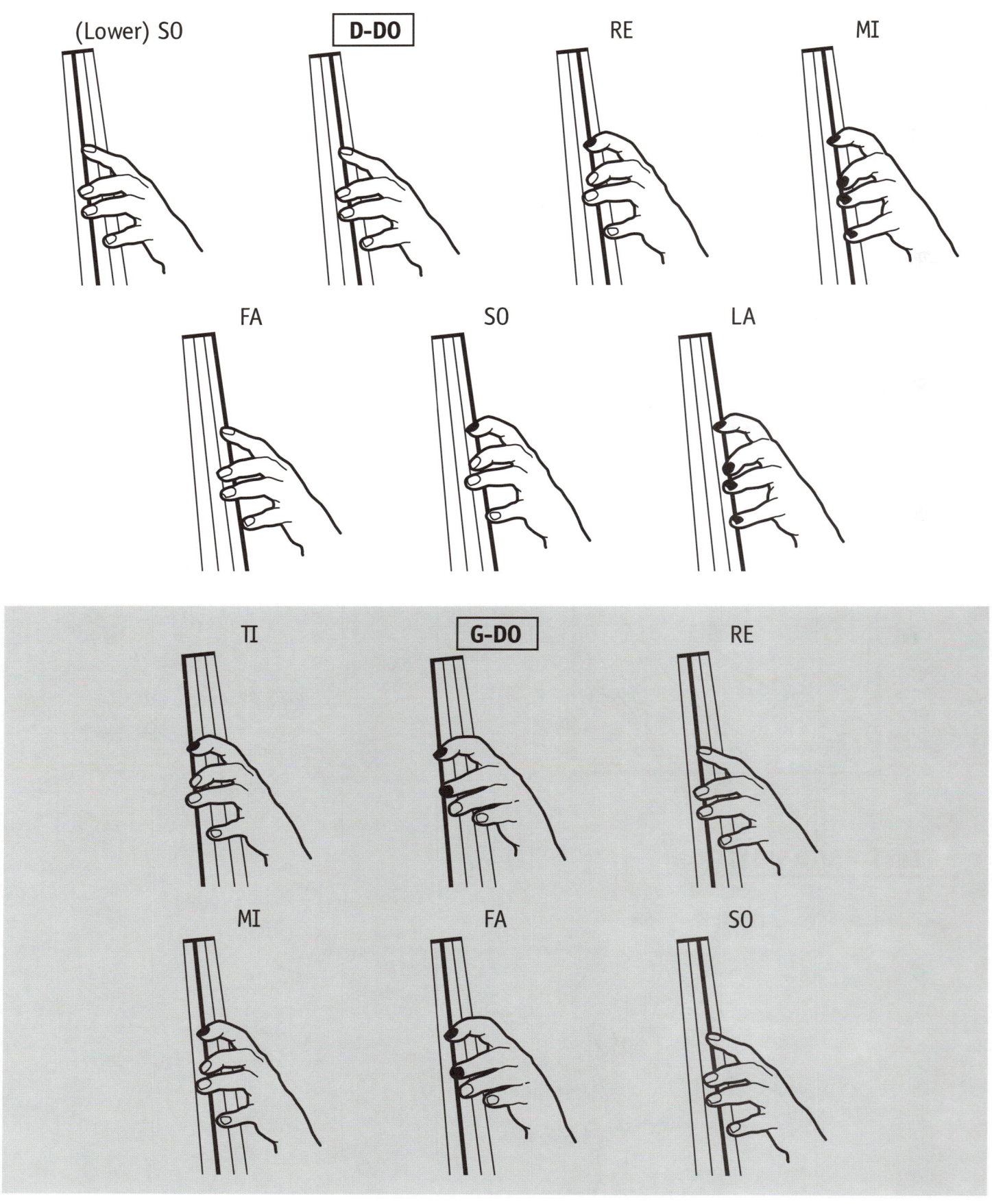

BASS FINGERINGS

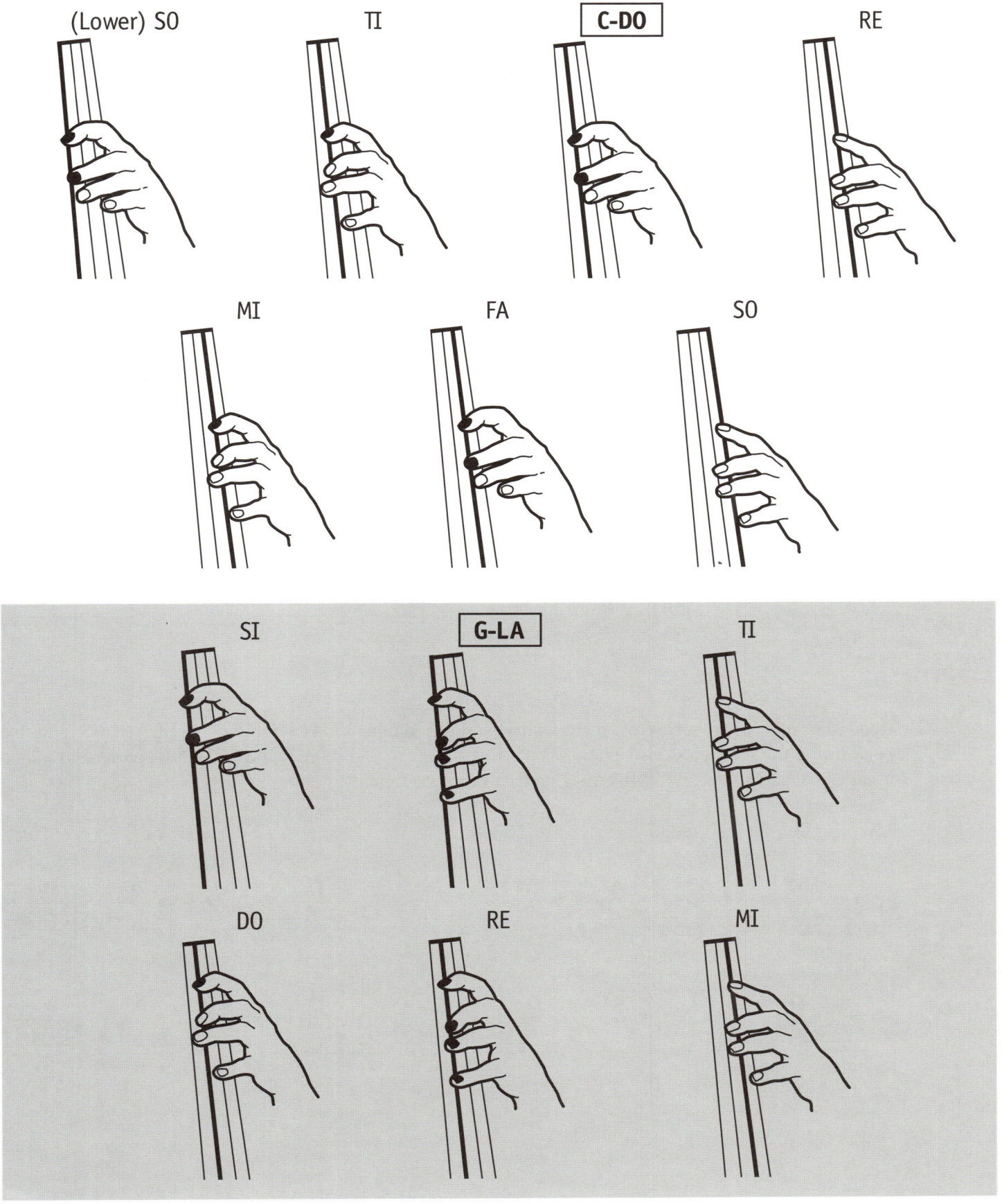

TONAL READING
TONIC AND DOMINANT FUNCTIONS IN D MAJOR

1. Read the following patterns by singing them WITH TONAL SYLLABLES and by performing them on your instrument. The arrow points to DO. D indicates a TONIC pattern in major tonality; A7 indicates a DOMINANT pattern in major tonality.

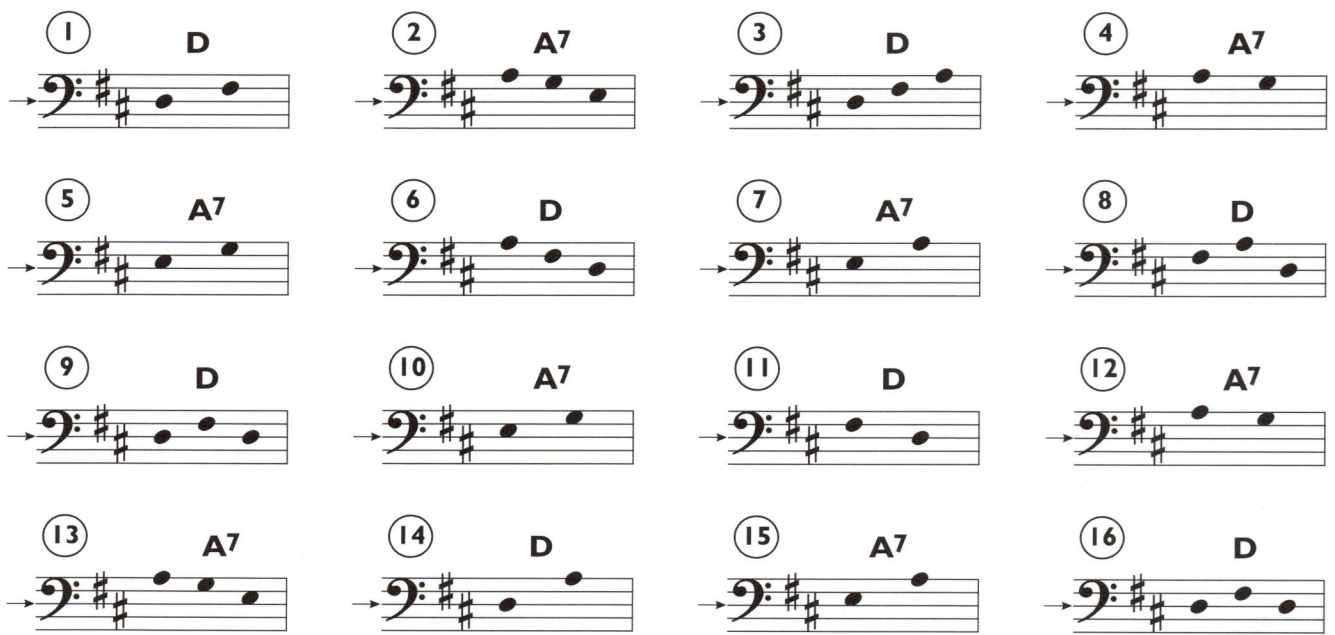

2. Read the following series of patterns by singing them WITH TONAL SYLLABLES and by performing them on your instrument. The arrow points to DO. D indicates a TONIC pattern in major tonality; A7 indicates a DOMINANT pattern in major tonality.

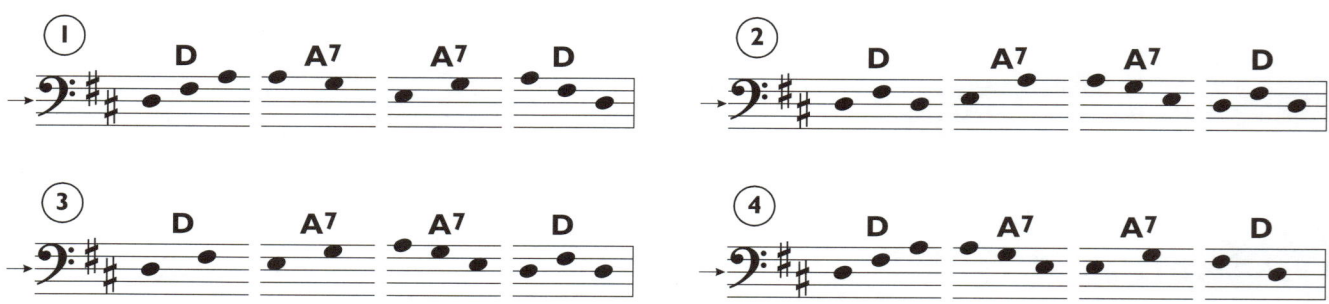

Be expressive when performing with your voice and with your instrument!

RHYTHM READING
MACROBEATS AND MICROBEATS IN DUPLE METER

1. Read the following patterns by chanting them WITH RHYTHM SYLLABLES and by performing them on your instrument.

   The number (2) tells how many macrobeats there are in a measure.
   The symbol (♩) indicates the kind of note that is a macrobeat.

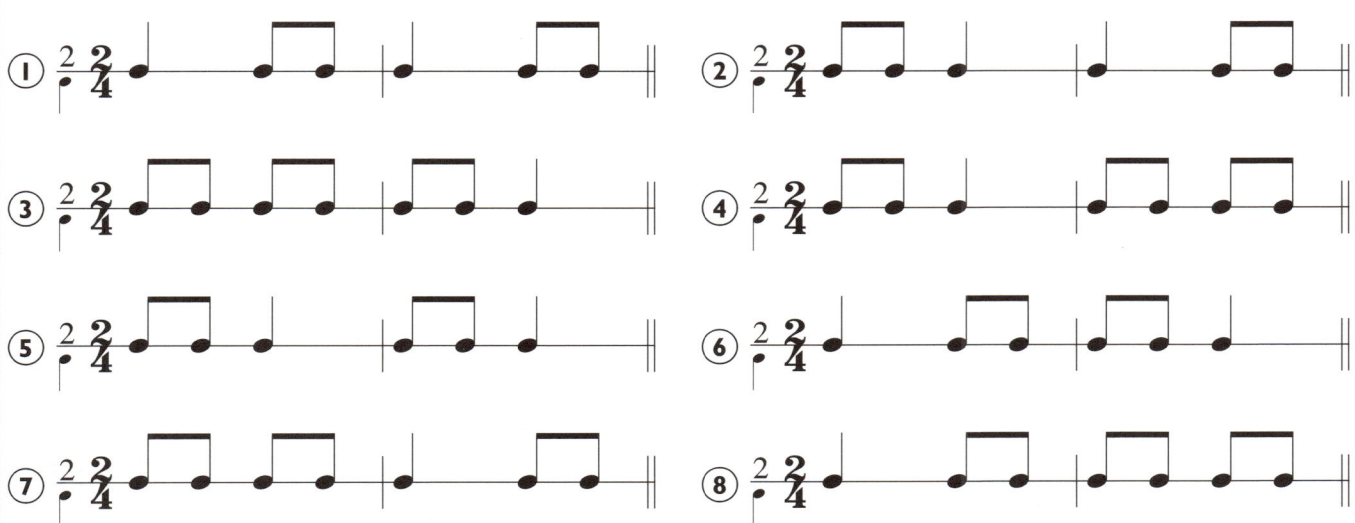

2. Read the following series of patterns by chanting them WITH RHYTHM SYLLABLES and by performing them on your instrument.

   The number (2) tells how many macrobeats there are in a measure.
   The symbol (♩) indicates the kind of note that is a macrobeat.

Be expressive when performing with your voice and with your instrument!

HOT CROSS BUNS

MARY HAD A LITTLE LAMB

TWINKLE, TWINKLE, LITTLE STAR

TONAL READING
TONIC AND DOMINANT FUNCTIONS IN G MAJOR

1. Read the following patterns by singing them WITH TONAL SYLLABLES and by performing them on your instrument. The arrow points to DO. G indicates a TONIC pattern in major tonality; D7 indicates a DOMINANT pattern in major tonality.

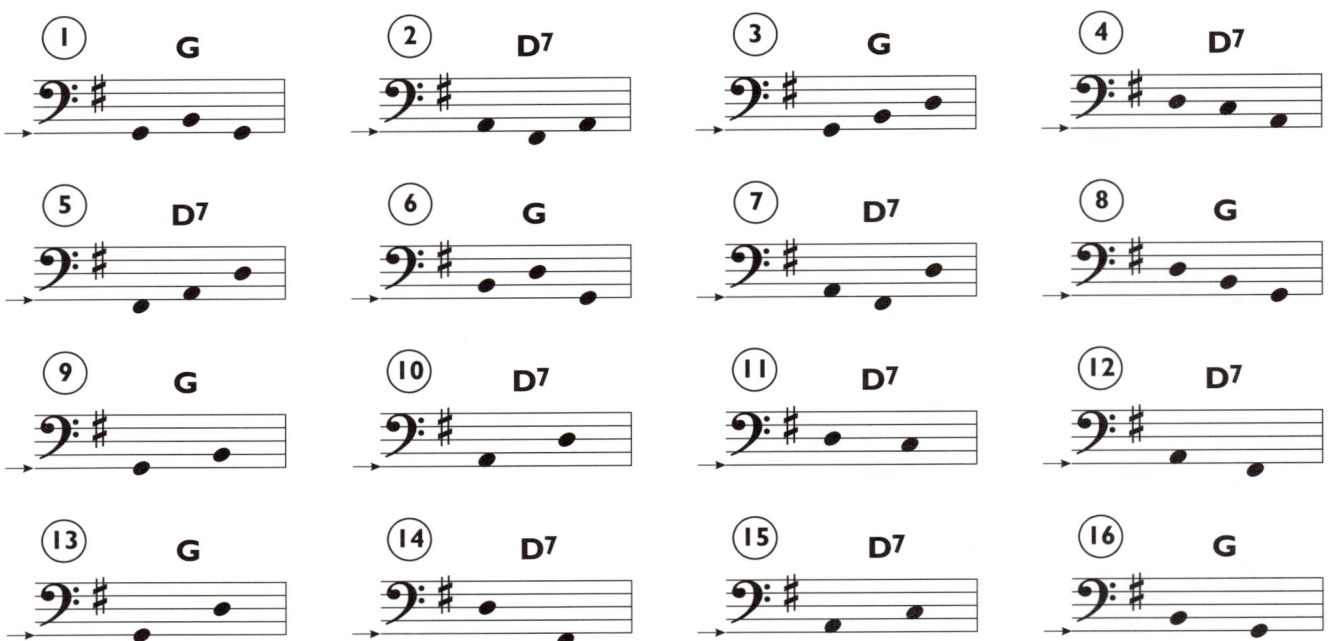

2. Read the following series of patterns by singing them WITH TONAL SYLLABLES and by performing them on your instrument. The arrow points to DO. G indicates a TONIC pattern in major tonality; D7 indicates a DOMINANT pattern in major tonality.

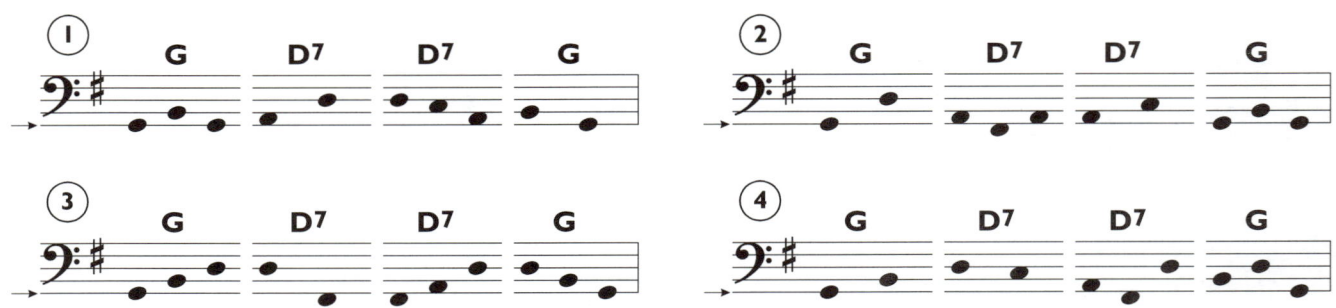

Be expressive when performing with your voice and with your instrument!

TONAL READING
TONIC, DOMINANT, AND SUBDOMINANT FUNCTIONS IN G MAJOR

1. Read the following patterns by singing them WITH TONAL SYLLABLES and by performing them on your instrument. The arrow points to DO. G indicates a TONIC pattern in major tonality; D7 indicates a DOMINANT pattern in major tonality; and C indicates a SUBDOMINANT pattern in major tonality.

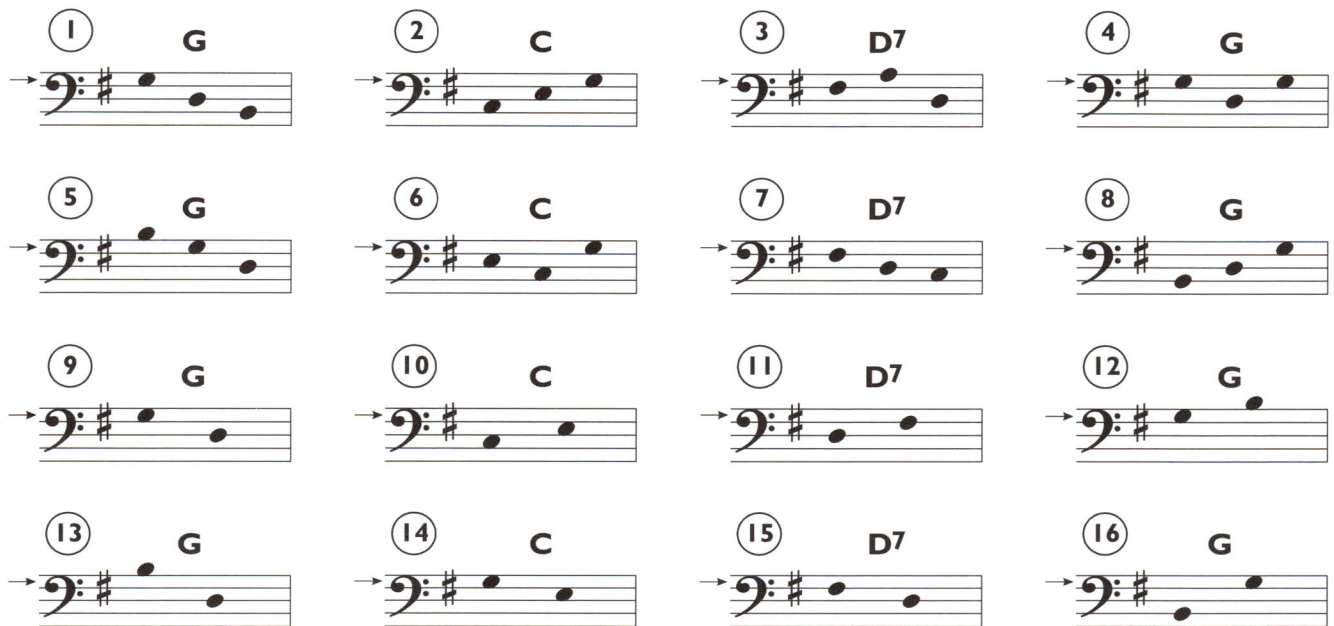

2. Read the following series of patterns by singing them WITH TONAL SYLLABLES and by performing them on your instrument. The arrow points to DO. G indicates a TONIC pattern in major tonality; D7 indicates a DOMINANT pattern in major tonality; and C indicates a SUBDOMINANT pattern in major tonality.

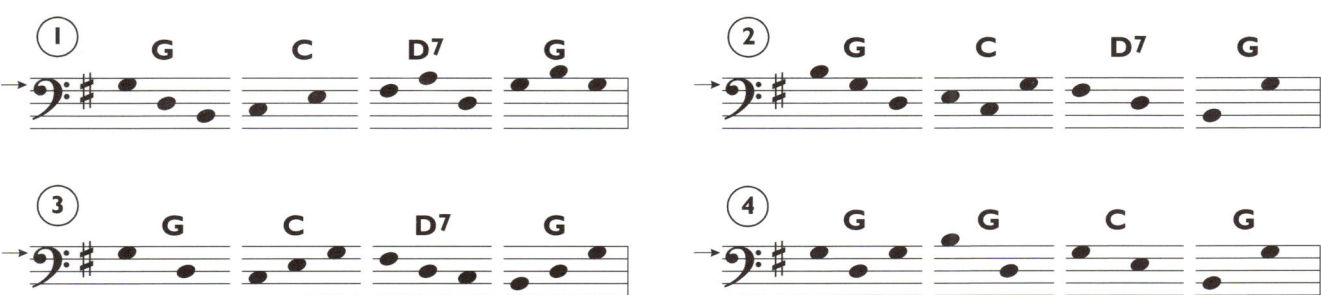

Be expressive when performing with your voice and with your instrument!

MAJOR DUPLE

RHYTHM READING
MACROBEATS AND MICROBEATS IN TRIPLE METER

1. Read the following patterns by chanting them WITH RHYTHM SYLLABLES and by performing them on your instrument.

   The number (2) tells how many macrobeats there are in a measure.
   The symbol (♩·) indicates the kind of note that is a macrobeat.

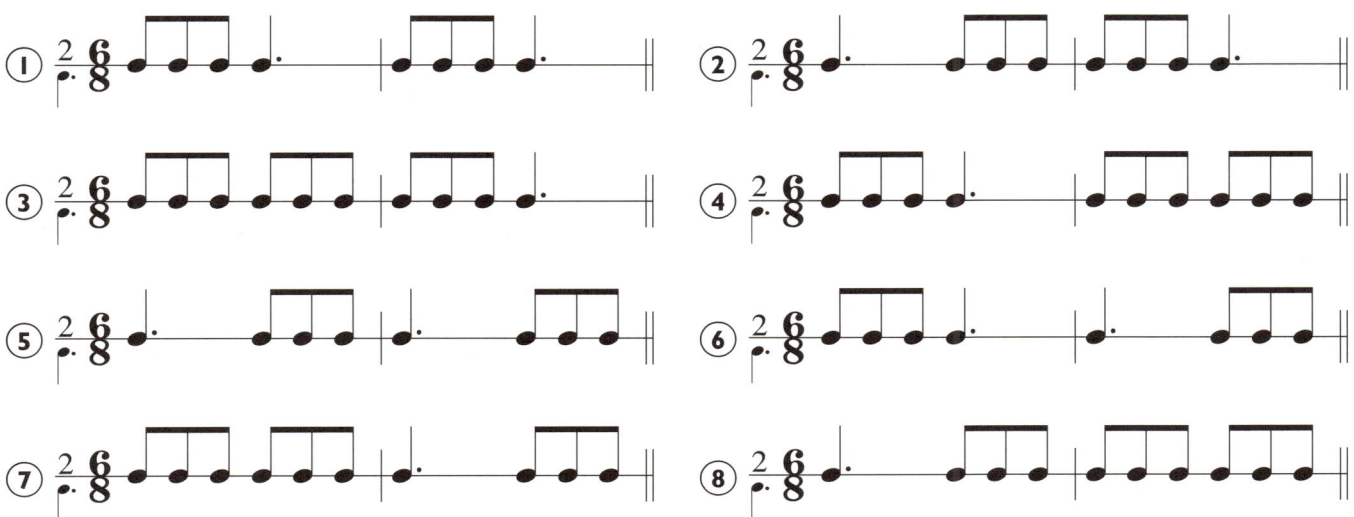

2. Read the following series of patterns by chanting them WITH RHYTHM SYLLABLES and by performing them on your instrument.

   The number (2) tells how many macrobeats there are in a measure.
   The symbol (♩·) indicates the kind of note that is a macrobeat.

Be expressive when performing with your voice and with your instrument!

MAJOR TRIPLE

ENRHYTHMIC READING
MACROBEATS AND MICROBEATS IN DUPLE METER

1. Read the following patterns by chanting them WITH RHYTHM SYLLABLES and by performing them on your instrument. The patterns on the left (4/4) are enrhythmic (they sound the same, but look different) with the patterns on the right (¢).

   The numbers (4, 2) indicate how many macrobeats are in a measure.
   The symbols (♩ , ♩) indicate the kind of note that is a macrobeat.

Be expressive when performing with your voice and with your instrument!

MAJOR DUPLE

TONAL READING
TONIC AND DOMINANT FUNCTIONS IN C MAJOR

1. Read the following patterns by singing them WITH TONAL SYLLABLES and by performing them on your instrument. The arrow points to DO. C indicates a TONIC pattern in major tonality; G7 indicates a DOMINANT pattern in major tonality.

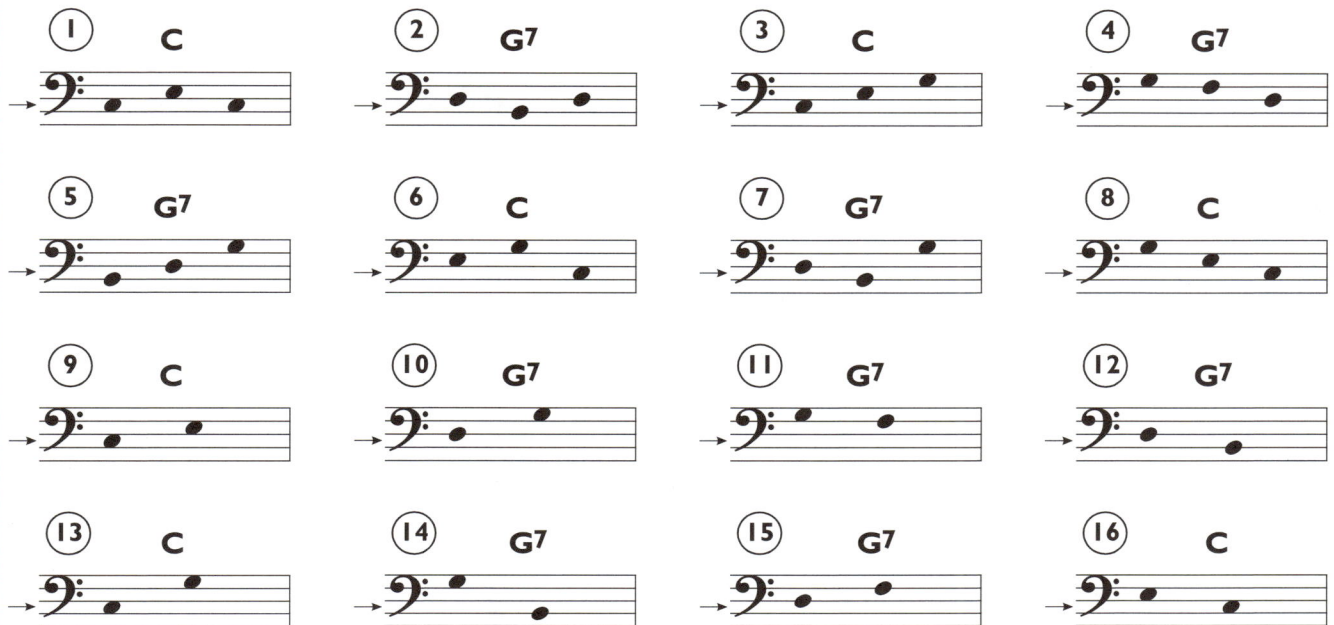

2. Read the following series of patterns by singing them WITH TONAL SYLLABLES and by performing them on your instrument. The arrow points to DO. C indicates a TONIC pattern in major tonality; G7 indicates a DOMINANT pattern in major tonality.

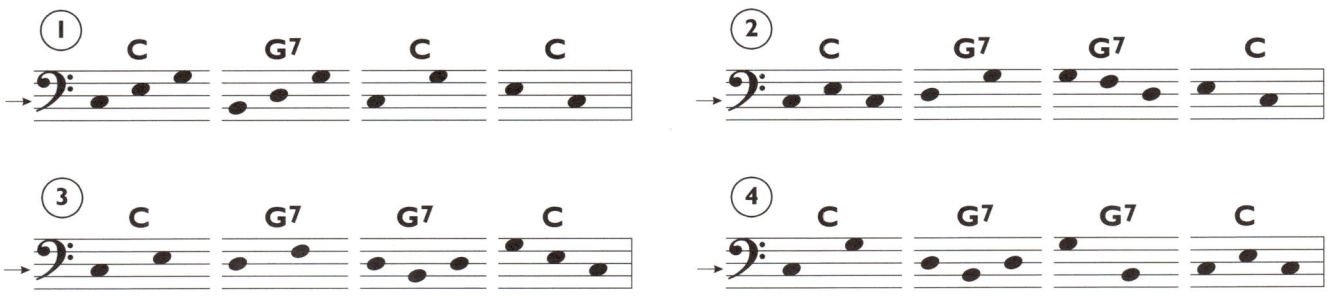

Be expressive when performing with your voice and with your instrument!

TONAL READING
TONIC, DOMINANT, AND SUBDOMINANT FUNCTIONS IN C MAJOR

1. Read the following patterns by singing them WITH TONAL SYLLABLES and by performing them on your instrument. The arrow points to DO. C indicates a TONIC pattern in major tonality; G7 indicates a DOMINANT pattern in major tonality; and F indicates a SUBDOMINANT pattern in major tonality.

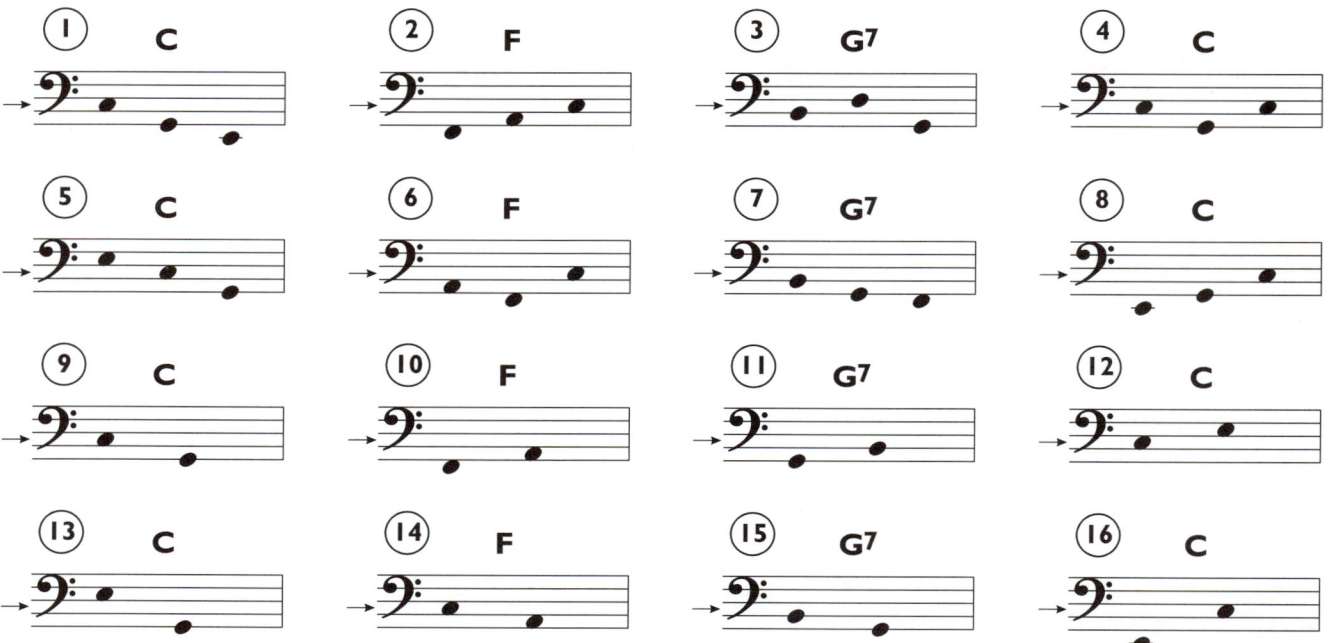

2. Read the following series of patterns by singing them WITH TONAL SYLLABLES and by performing them on your instrument. The arrow points to DO. C indicates a TONIC pattern in major tonality; G7 indicates a DOMINANT pattern in major tonality; and F indicates a SUBDOMINANT pattern in major tonality.

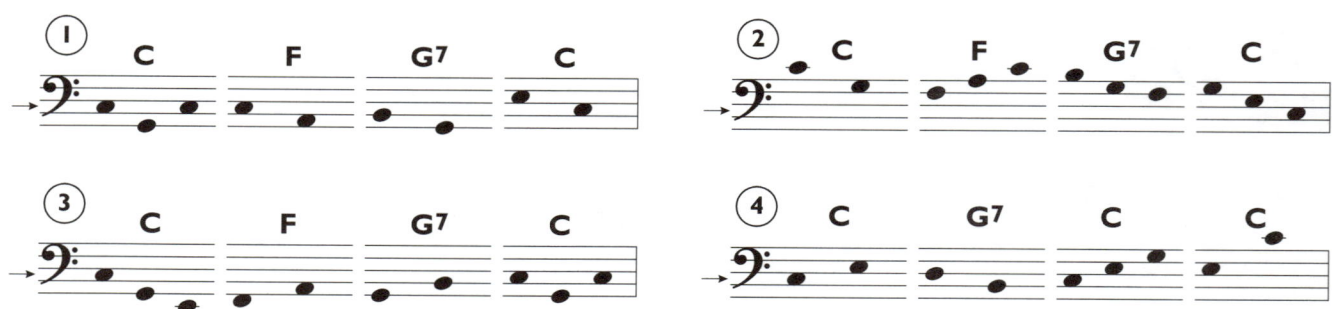

Be expressive when performing with your voice and with your instrument!

ENRHYTHMIC READING
MACROBEATS AND MICROBEATS IN TRIPLE METER

1. Read the following patterns by chanting them WITH RHYTHM SYLLABLES and by performing them on your instrument. The patterns on the left (3/8) are enrhythmic (they sound the same, but look different) with the patterns on the right (3/4).

   The numbers (1, 1) indicate how many macrobeats are in a measure.
   The symbols (♩· , ♩·) indicate the kind of note that is a macrobeat.

Be expressive when performing with your voice and with your instrument!

MAJOR TRIPLE

RHYTHM READING
MACROBEATS, MICROBEATS, AND DIVISIONS IN DUPLE METER

1. Read the following patterns by chanting them WITH RHYTHM SYLLABLES and by performing them on your instrument.

   The number (2) tells how many macrobeats there are in a measure.
   The symbol (♩) indicates the kind of note that is a macrobeat.

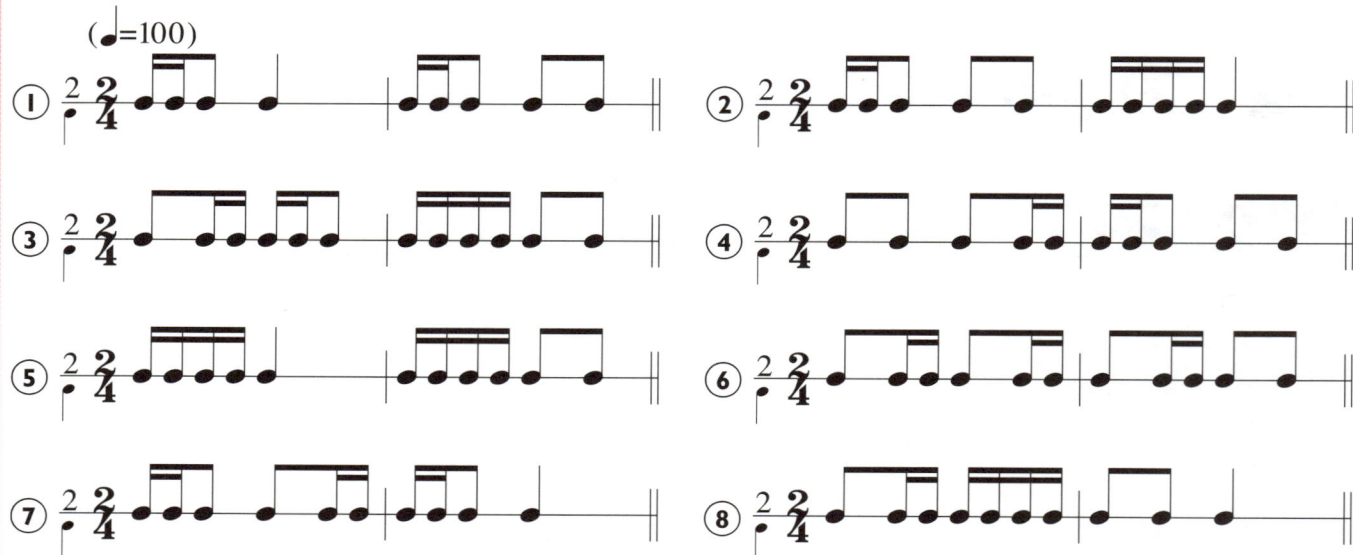

2. Read the following series of patterns by chanting them WITH RHYTHM SYLLABLES and by performing them on your instrument.

   The number (2) tells how many macrobeats there are in a measure.
   The symbol (♩) indicates the kind of note that is a macrobeat.

Be expressive when performing with your voice and with your instrument!

DOWN BY THE STATION

TONAL READING
TONIC AND DOMINANT FUNCTIONS IN G MINOR

1. Read the following patterns by singing them WITH TONAL SYLLABLES and by performing them on your instrument. The arrow points to DO. Gm indicates a TONIC pattern in minor tonality; D7 indicates a DOMINANT pattern in minor tonality.

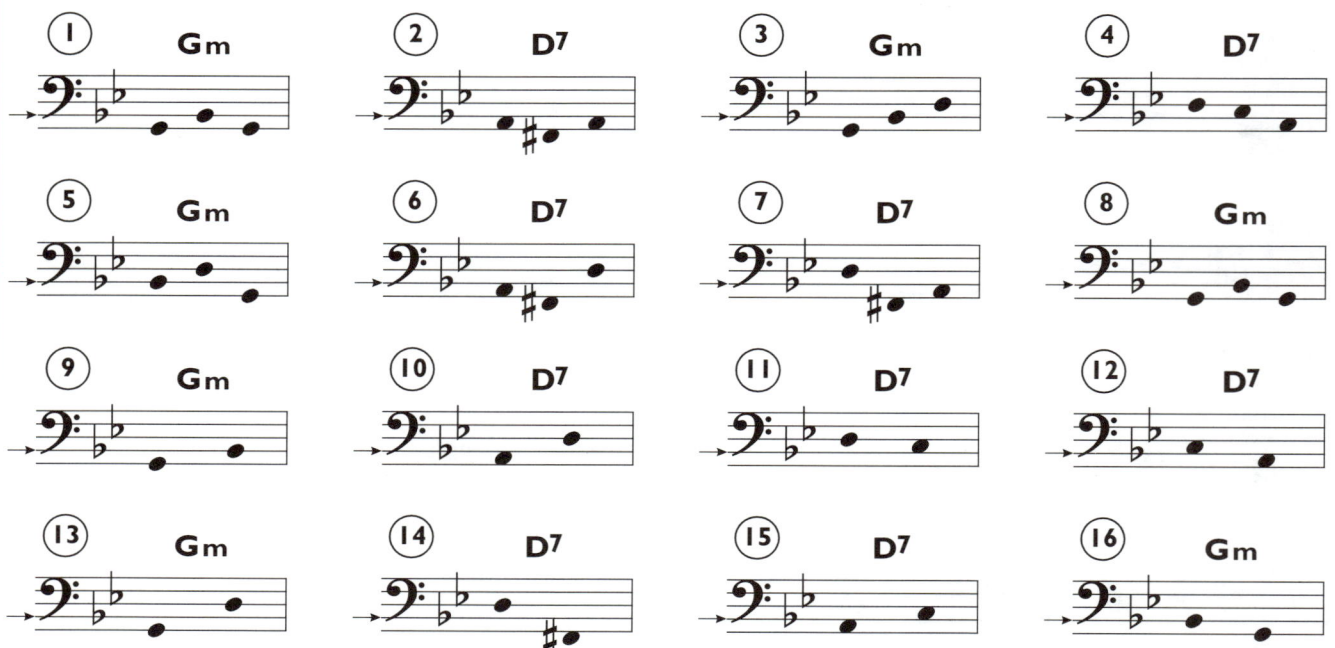

2. Read the following series of patterns by singing them WITH TONAL SYLLABLES and by performing them on your instrument. The arrow points to DO. Gm indicates a TONIC pattern in minor tonality; D7 indicates a DOMINANT pattern in minor tonality.

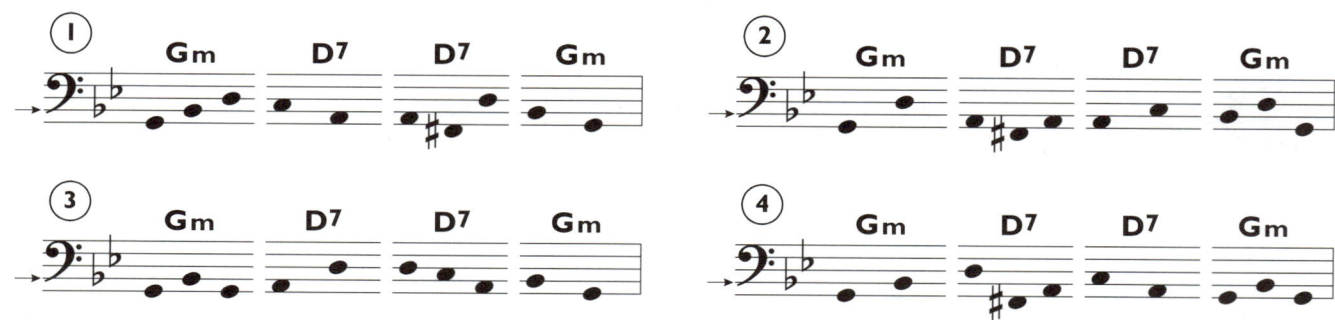

Be expressive when performing with your voice and with your instrument!

MINOR DUPLE

MINOR TRIPLE

ENRHYTHMIC READING
MACROBEATS, MICROBEATS, AND DIVISIONS IN DUPLE METER

1. Read the following patterns by chanting them WITH RHYTHM SYLLABLES and by performing them on your instrument. The patterns on the left (4/4) are enrhythmic (they sound the same, but look different) with the patterns on the right (₵).

   The numbers (4, 2) indicate how many macrobeats are in a measure.
   The symbols (♩ , ♪) indicate the kind of note that is a macrobeat.

Be expressive when performing with your voice and with your instrument!

RHYTHM READING
MACROBEATS, MICROBEATS, AND DIVISIONS IN TRIPLE METER

1. Read the following patterns by chanting them WITH RHYTHM SYLLABLES and by performing them on your instrument.

   The number (2) tells how many macrobeats there are in a measure.
   The symbol (♩.) indicates the kind of note that is a macrobeat.

2. Read the following series of patterns by chanting them WITH RHYTHM SYLLABLES and by performing them on your instrument.

   The number (2) tells how many macrobeats there are in a measure.
   The symbol (♩.) indicates the kind of note that is a macrobeat.

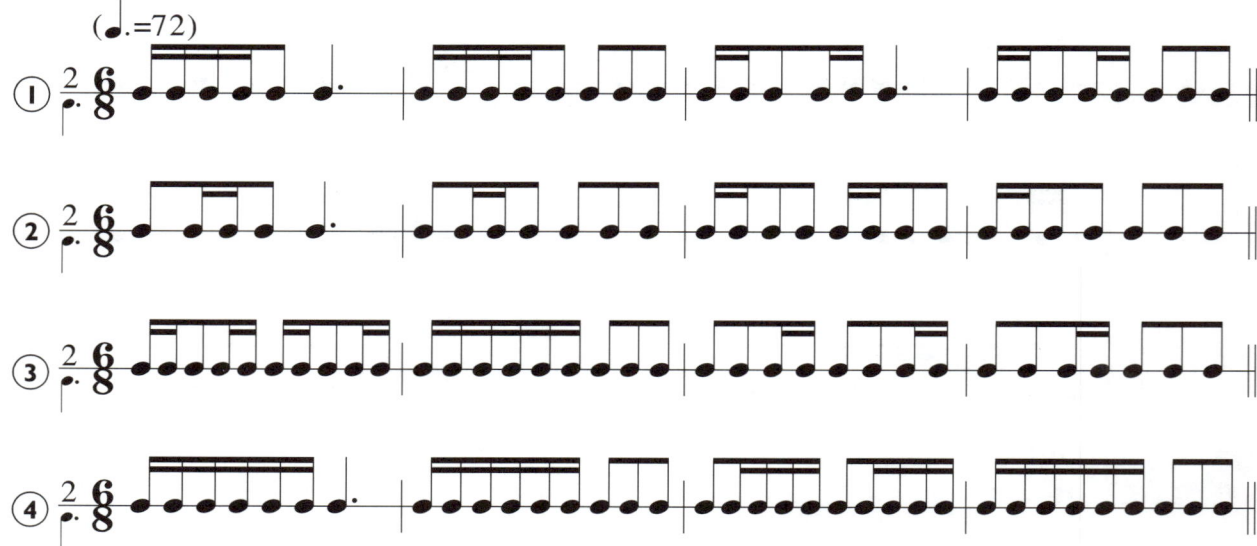

Be expressive when performing with your voice and with your instrument!

ENRHYTHMIC READING
MACROBEATS, MICROBEATS, AND DIVISIONS IN TRIPLE METER

1. Read the following patterns by chanting them WITH RHYTHM SYLLABLES and by performing them on your instrument. The patterns on the left (3/8) are enrhythmic (they sound the same, but look different) with the patterns on the right (3/4).

   The numbers (1, 1) indicate how many macrobeats are in a measure.
   The symbols (♩· , ♪·) indicate the kind of note that is a macrobeat.

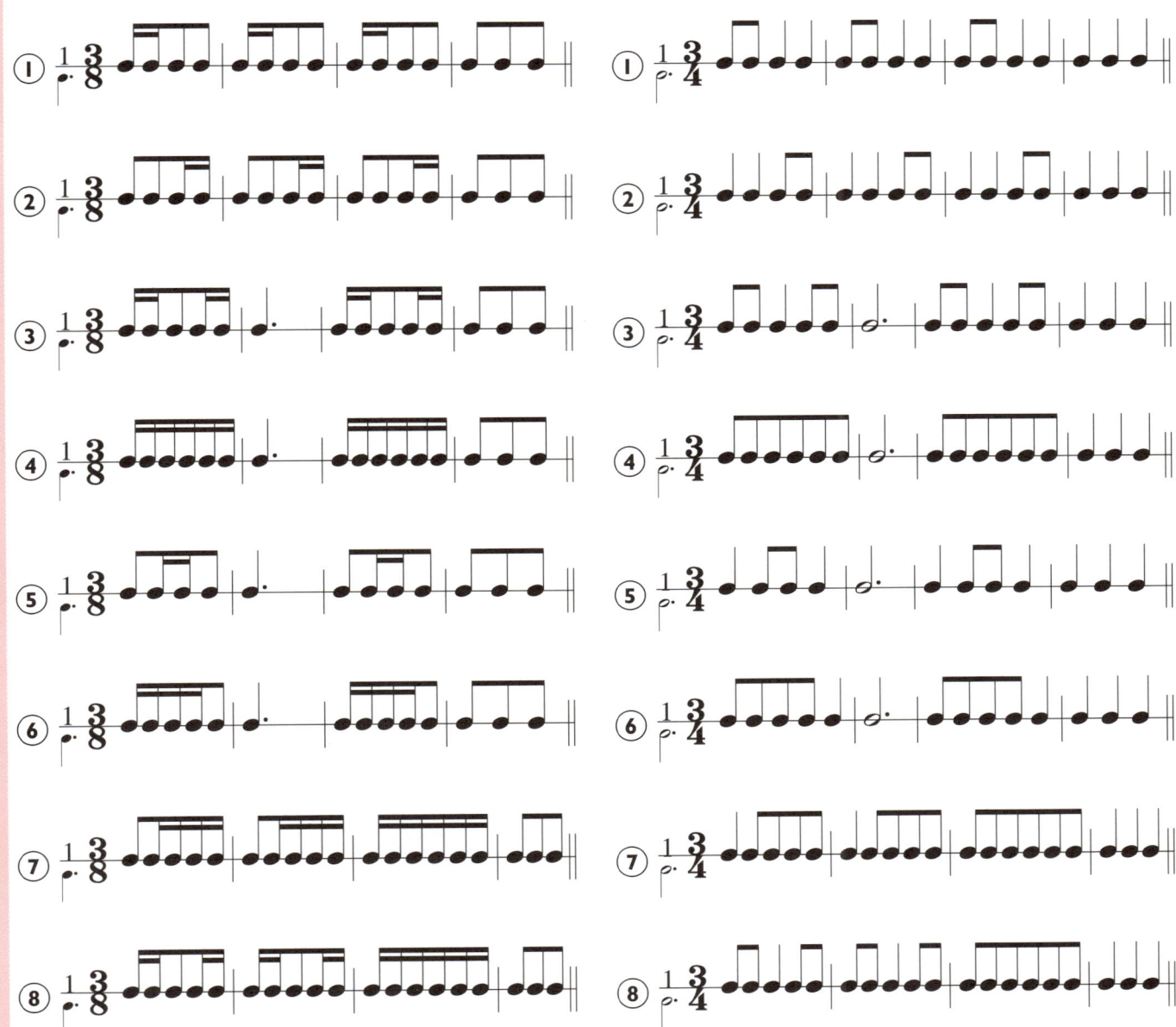

Be expressive when performing with your voice and with your instrument!

TRIPLE TWINKLE

RHYTHM READING
MACROBEATS, MICROBEATS, DIVISIONS, AND ELONGATIONS IN DUPLE METER

1. Read the following patterns by chanting them WITH RHYTHM SYLLABLES and by performing them on your instrument.

   The number (2) tells how many macrobeats there are in a measure.
   The symbol (♩) indicates the kind of note that is a macrobeat.

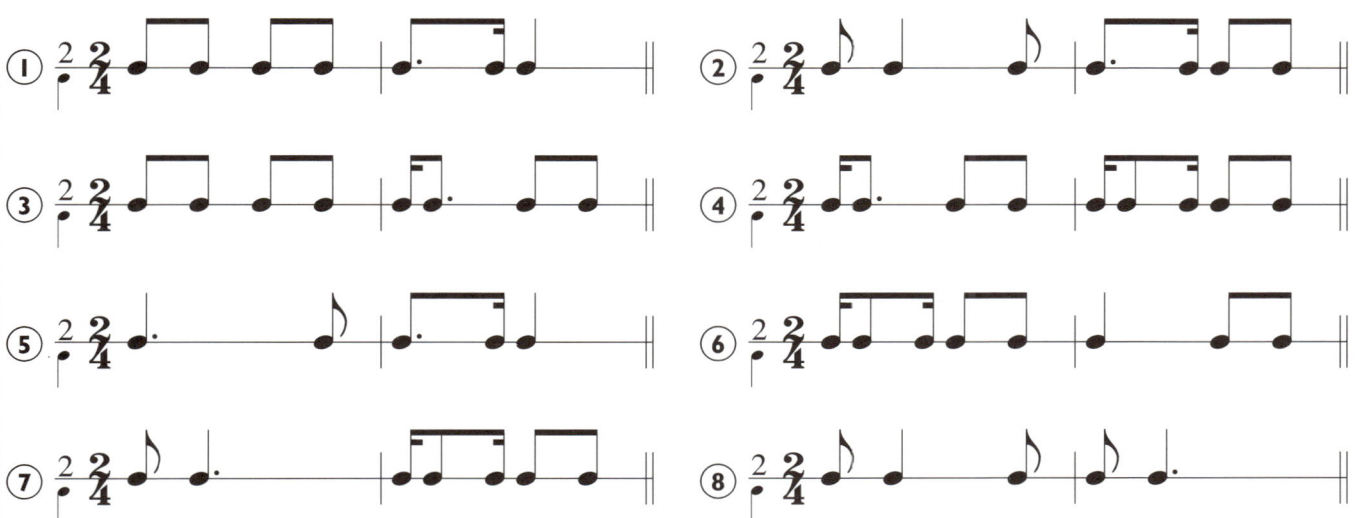

2. Read the following series of patterns by chanting them WITH RHYTHM SYLLABLES and by performing them on your instrument.

   The number (2) tells how many macrobeats there are in a measure.
   The symbol (♩) indicates the kind of note that is a macrobeat.

Be expressive when performing with your voice and with your instrument!

ENRHYTHMIC READING
MACROBEATS, MICROBEATS, DIVISIONS, AND ELONGATIONS IN DUPLE METER

1. Read the following patterns by chanting them WITH RHYTHM SYLLABLES and by performing them on your instrument. The patterns on the left (4/4) are enrhythmic (they sound the same, but look different) with the patterns on the right (₵).

   The numbers (4, 2) indicate how many macrobeats are in a measure.
   The symbols (♩ , ♩) indicate the kind of note that is a macrobeat.

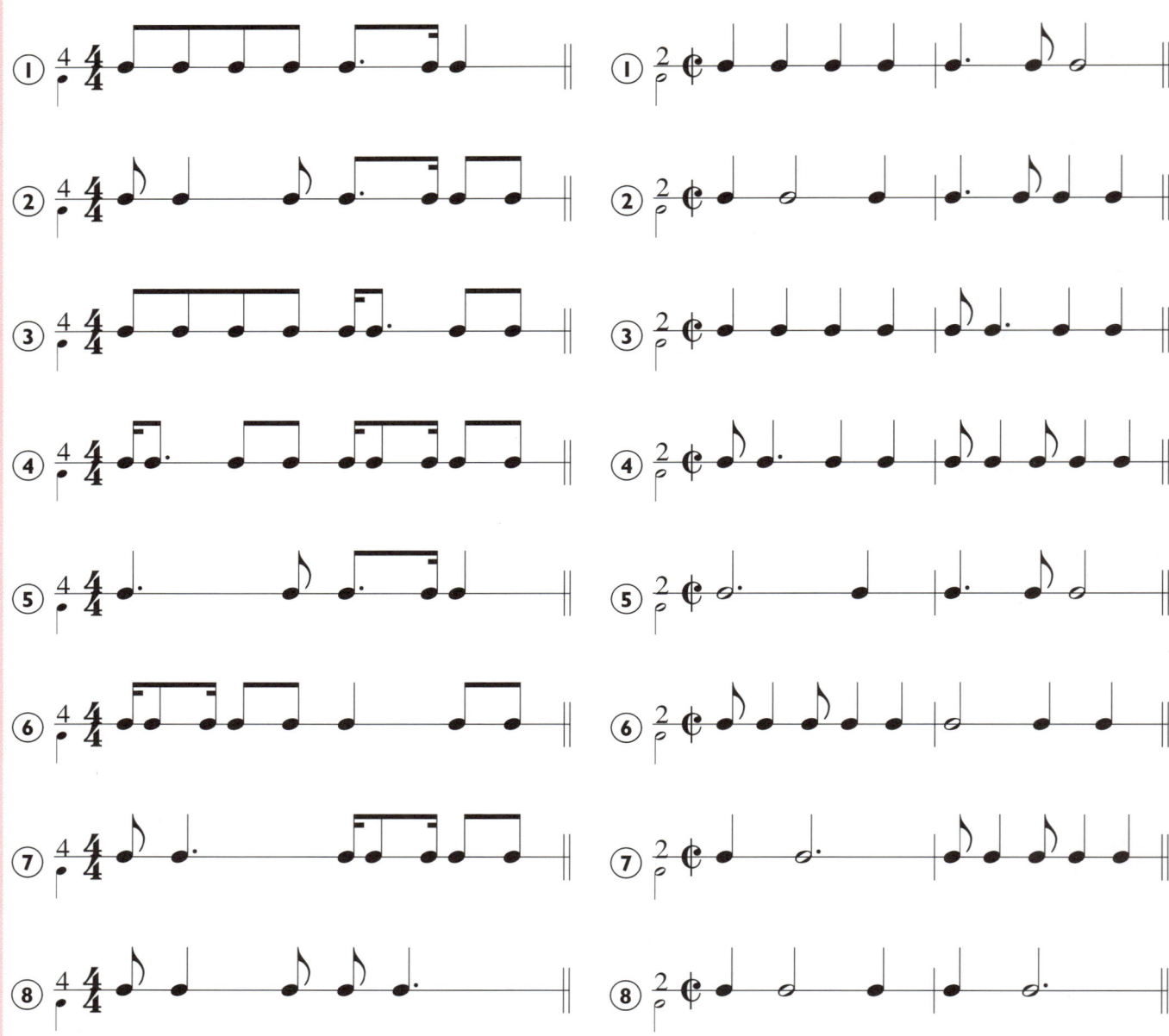

Be expressive when performing with your voice and with your instrument!

LIGHTLY ROW

TRIPLE PIERROT

GO TELL AUNT RHODY

RHYTHM READING
MACROBEATS, MICROBEATS, DIVISIONS, AND ELONGATIONS IN TRIPLE METER

1. Read the following patterns by chanting them WITH RHYTHM SYLLABLES and by performing them on your instrument.

   The number (2) tells how many macrobeats there are in a measure.
   The symbol (♩·) indicates the kind of note that is a macrobeat.

2. Read the following series of patterns by chanting them WITH RHYTHM SYLLABLES and by performing them on your instrument.

   The number (2) tells how many macrobeats there are in a measure.
   The symbol (♩·) indicates the kind of note that is a macrobeat.

Be expressive when performing with your voice and with your instrument!

ENRHYTHMIC READING
MACROBEATS, MICROBEATS, DIVISIONS, AND ELONGATIONS IN TRIPLE METER

1. Read the following patterns by chanting them WITH RHYTHM SYLLABLES and by performing them on your instrument. The patterns on the left (3/8) are enrhythmic (they sound the same, but look different) with the patterns on the right (3/4).

   The numbers (1, 1) indicate how many macrobeats are in a measure.
   The symbols (♩. , ♩.) indicate the kind of note that is a macrobeat.

Be expressive when performing with your voice and with your instrument!

LITTLE TOM TINKER

MINOR AUNT RHODY

BAA, BAA, BLACK SHEEP

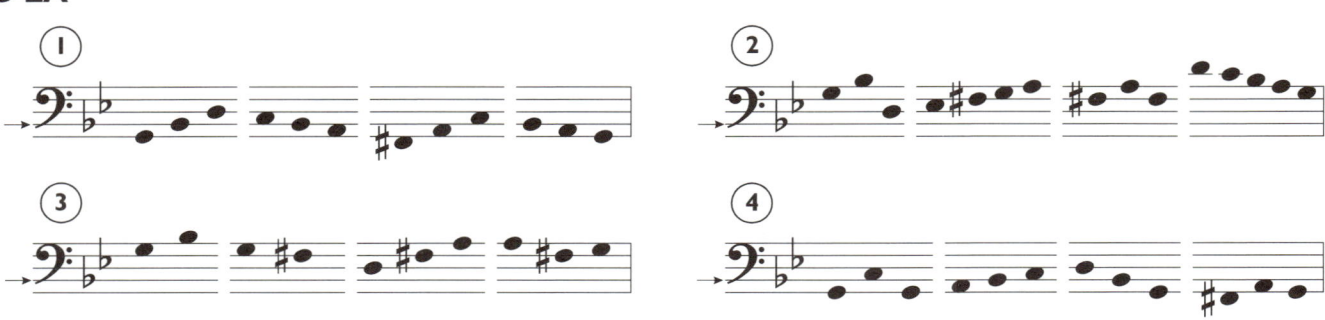

TONAL SIGHT READING

1. Sight read the following patterns by singing them WITH A NEUTRAL SYLLABLE and by performing them on your instrument. Some of the patterns are familiar and some are unfamiliar. The arrow points to DO.

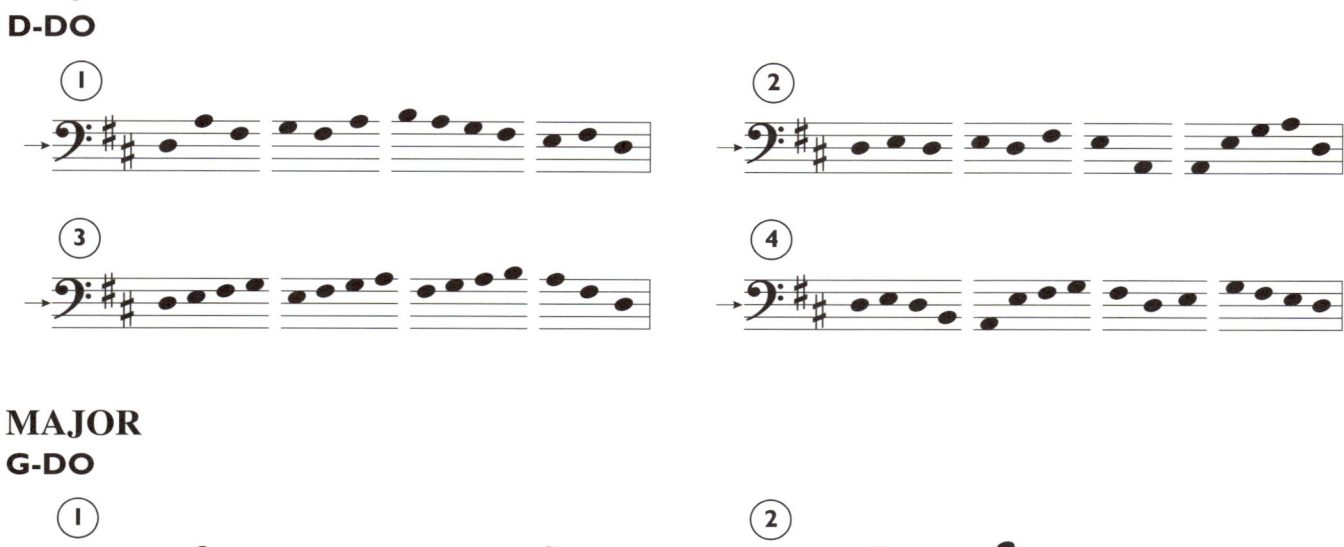

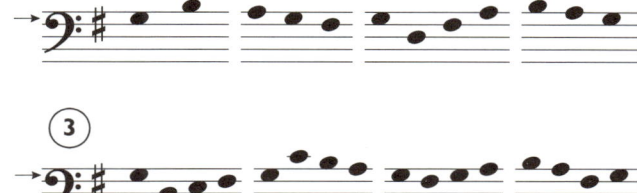

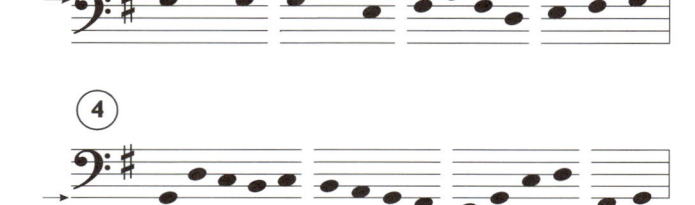

MAJOR
D-DO

MAJOR
G-DO

MAJOR
C-DO

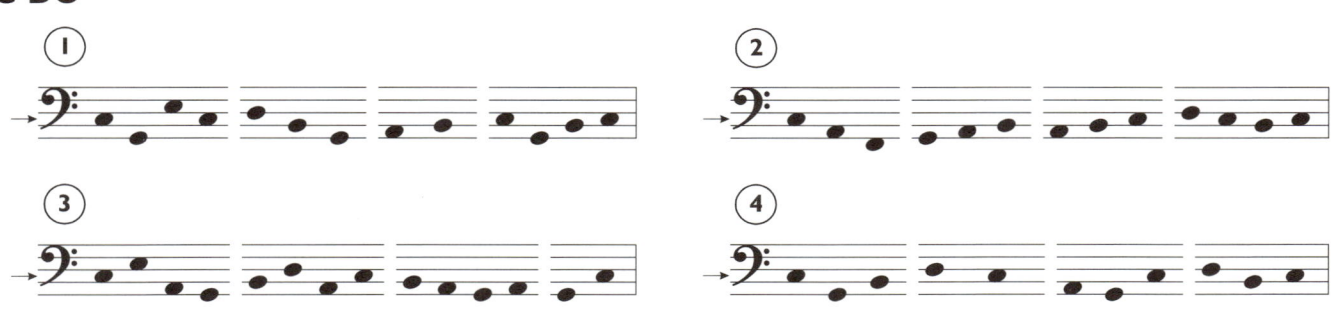

MINOR
G-LA

RHYTHM SIGHT READING

1. Sight read the following rhythm patterns by chanting them WITH A NEUTRAL SYLLABLE and by performing them on your instrument. Some of the patterns are familiar and some are unfamiliar.

   The number (2) tells how many macrobeats there are in a measure.
   The symbol (♩ or ♩·) indicates the kind of note that is a macrobeat.

DUPLE

TRIPLE

RHYTHM SIGHT READING (continued)

DUPLE

TRIPLE

MELODIC SIGHT READING

1. Audiate one of the following melodies. If necessary, SING INDIVIDUAL TONAL PATTERNS WITH TONAL SYLLABLES, and CHANT INDIVIDUAL RHYTHM PATTERNS WITH RHYTHM SYLLABLES. DO NOT SING THE ENTIRE MELODY WITH TONAL SYLLABLES. YOU MAY CHANT THE ENTIRE MELODIC RHYTHM USING RHYTHM SYLLABLES.

2. Audiate that melody while performing it silently on your instrument.

3. Perform that melody on your instrument.

MUSICAL ENRICHMENT

"Musical Enrichment" begins with item #94 on the *Home-Study Compact Disc*. Listen Carefully as a professional musician performs some familiar folk songs. Before each performance the announcer will give the resting tone and starting pitch. For example:

"G is DO, start on DO," indicates that
1) G is the resting tone,
2) the song is in major tonality (because DO is the resting tone), and
3) the song begins on DO.

"G is LA, start on MI," indicates that
1) G is the resting tone,
2) the song is in minor tonality (because LA is the resting tone), and
3) the song begins on MI.

Listen many times to the songs, noting the tone quality, style of articulation, and phrasing. When you can audiate a song (when you can hear it in your head), you may begin to perform that song "by ear." Some of the songs are easy and will require little time to learn to perform. Other songs are more challenging and will require more time to learn to perform. The fingering chart beginning on the next page will help you locate the appropriate DO or LA, and the correct starting pitch. Remember it is alright to make mistakes when you first play "by ear."

Musical Enrichment also includes the activities listed below. Your music teacher will help you mark the charts to indicate when you have satisfactorily completed each of the activities.

A. Sing the song with or without words.
B. Perform the song in the tonality and keyality found on the *Home-Study Compact Disc*.
C. Perform the song in a different keyality. (Start on a different note.)
D. Perform the song with a friend who plays the same or a different instrument.
E. Perform the song in a different meter. (Change from duple to triple or from triple to duple.)
F. Perform the song in a different tonality. (Change from major to minor or from minor to major.)
G. Perform an improvisation or harmony part for the song.

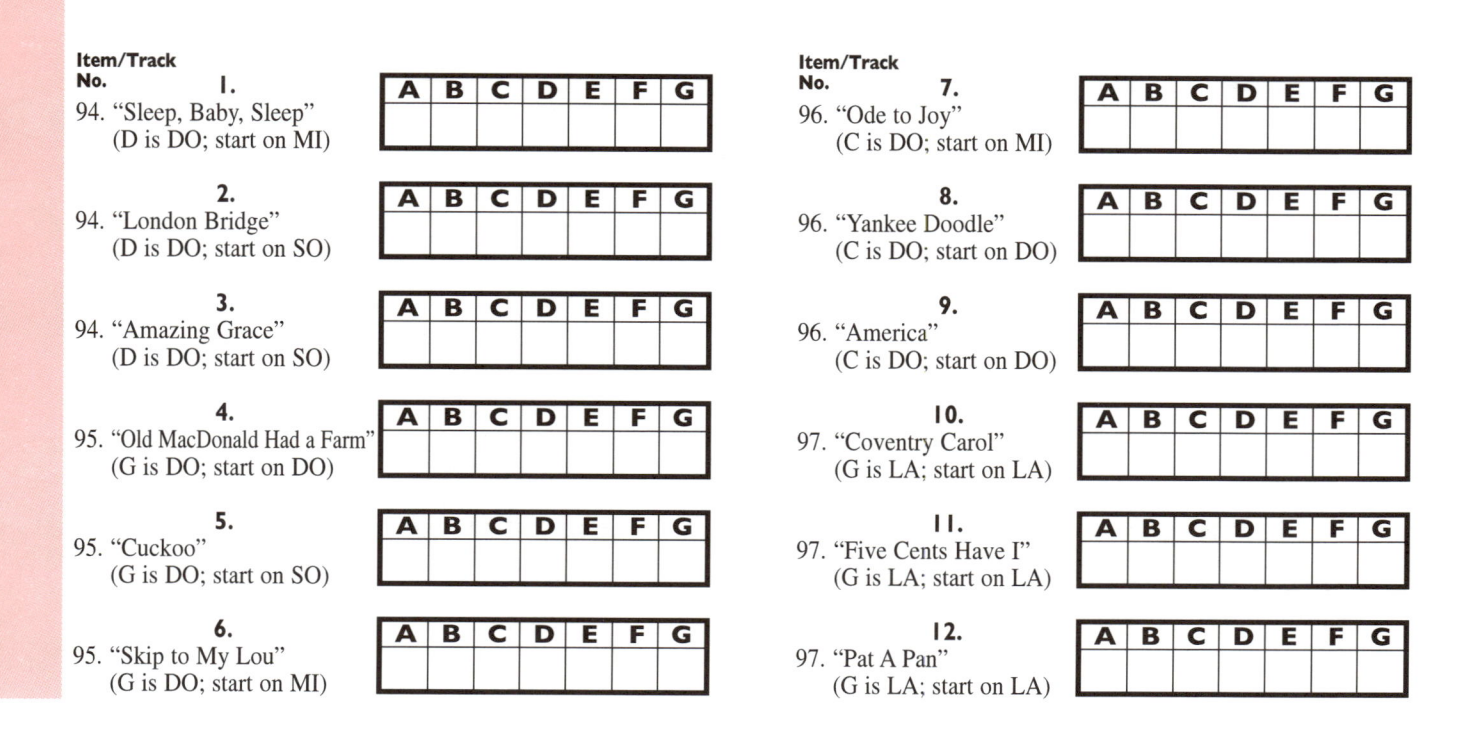

Item/Track
No.
1. 94. "Sleep, Baby, Sleep" (D is DO; start on MI)
2. 94. "London Bridge" (D is DO; start on SO)
3. 94. "Amazing Grace" (D is DO; start on SO)
4. 95. "Old MacDonald Had a Farm" (G is DO; start on DO)
5. 95. "Cuckoo" (G is DO; start on SO)
6. 95. "Skip to My Lou" (G is DO; start on MI)

Item/Track
No.
7. 96. "Ode to Joy" (C is DO; start on MI)
8. 96. "Yankee Doodle" (C is DO; start on DO)
9. 96. "America" (C is DO; start on DO)
10. 97. "Coventry Carol" (G is LA; start on LA)
11. 97. "Five Cents Have I" (G is LA; start on LA)
12. 97. "Pat A Pan" (G is LA; start on LA)

BASS FINGERING CHART

D-DO

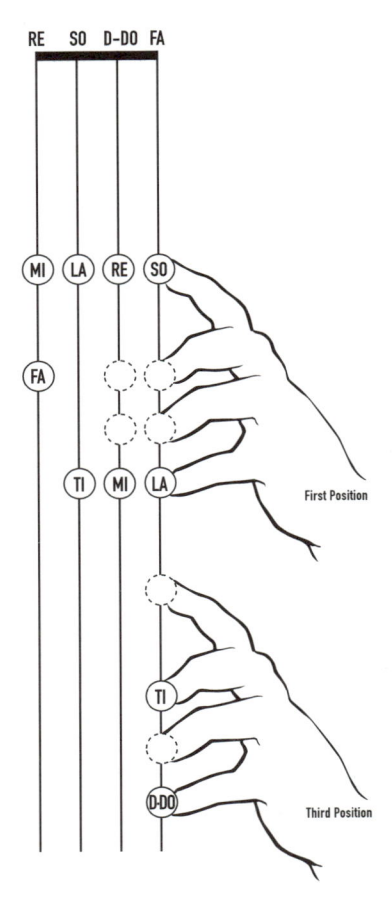

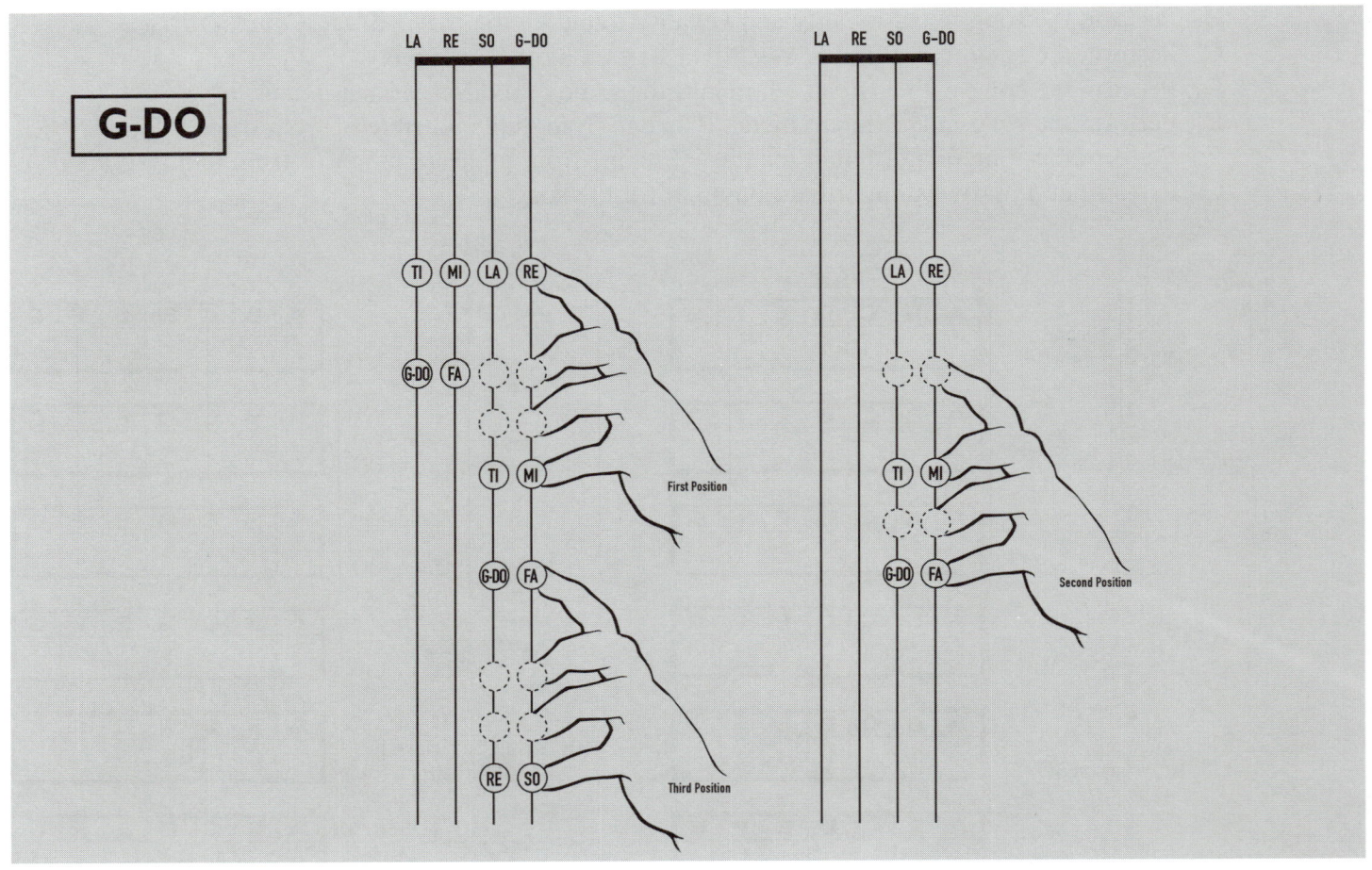

G-DO